cal **cozy** lovely gorgeous

creative smart

shable underfoo

nderfoot nosy lovely later

sed comical gorgeous dec

reative avid portable cau

noisy smart **noisy** entert

y voracious creative nosy

vely gorgeous eager natu

ve avid **new** cautious tal

al brave underfoot smart

nted nosy voracious gor

s decorative obsessed com
ble entertaining natural
e talented brave busy w
Different lovely talented t
art decorative smart obse
inseparable entertaining
uisitive natural washable
t lovely talented brave co
obsessed comical brave t
ertaining decorative crea
trusting inquisitive nat
brave cozy busy lovely ta

photographs by sharon beals

what kittens are

CHRONICLE BOOKS

SAN FRANCISCO

for Sam

Printed in Hong Kong.

ISBN 0-8118-2077-7

Library of Congress Cataloging-in-Publication Data available.

Book and cover design: Alfredo Gregory
Composition: Gregory Design

Distributed in Canada by Raincoast Books, 8680 Cambie Street, Vancouver, B.C. V6P 6M9

10   9   8   7   6   5   4   3   2   1

Chronicle Books
85 Second Street
San Francisco, CA 94105

www.chroniclebooks.com

kitten smitten   *I was in kitten heaven, but sadly, I had to leave. During the last three months of work on this book my world spilled with them. It was at least a kitten a day, either live or in a nostalgic darkroom reunion. (More than once I found myself fondly rubbing their little noses on the print.) At deadline time there were at least a dozen still tantalizing my brain, along with the wishful fantasy that my Chihuahua-pug would wag its tail at one instead of chasing it. And my ancient calico would give a welcoming trill, not a vehement hiss. So, obviously, for now I'll have to make do with the wonderful memories of the many makes, models, and styles of kittendom.* ▪ *All of them faster than Bambi at bundling themselves in our heart strings. All equally capable of producing poignantly pitched, undeniable, "rescue me" mews. All covered in touch-addicting softness, with fur so abundantly out-of-scale to their tiny bones. All capable of those convincing purrs that make anything else we're doing unimportant. All guaranteed a stay on our laps and shoulders. Did we have anything more important to do? (Kittens as the answer to the meaning of life.)* ▪ *Then you can add entertainment to the list of liking. Like a live nature show, those miniature cats-to-be. That's what they really are, despite starting out as small as —and only slightly more animated than —a prune. As soon as they attempt their first wobbly venture away from mom, they are doing some highly amusing but very serious homework for life as a cat. Only a chance of fate away from surviving in the wild,* everything, including the proverbial tail, *is new and must be explored, challenged, captured. Climbed, chewed, batted. Stalked intently: head low and paws stammering in courage-gathering fixation. Sprung upon with arch-backed, electric-furred, full-body pounces —thrill-a-minute living when instincts are working overtime to prepare those little bodies to survive in the wild realm of the living room.* ▪ *But mewing melodrama and biological brilliance can't completely explain their power to smite. The concept of bonding with a sweet little tabby or a cute little calico slides from maybe to yes faster than you can say "Siamese," not just because it's so hard to say no, but because it's so easy to say yes. Kittens are so do-able. (At least for those of you who don't have a cat-challenged dog at home.) Maybe it is that concentrated catness that does it: they come with fastidious genetics so the box is a snap, independence that liberates you from walks or kitty school, and just enough need for the tribe to end up purring on your pillow at night. Okay, I didn't mention the curtains, but how long does kittenhood last? Not long enough.*

new

decorative

c o m i c a l

gorgeous

entertaining

a   v   i   ∂

cautious

inquisitive

eager

t r u s t i n g

natural

washable

underfoot

s m a r t

daring

voracious

different

l o v e l y

t a l e n t e d

c   o   z   y

n o s y

acknowledgments *I am especially grateful to the Nob Hill Cat Clinic, Pets Unlimited, and the Oakland Animal Shelter for responding so enthusiastically to my requests for help in locating kittens. I'm in debt to all of the fosterers: Ann, Wendy, Julie and Natasha, Amy, Elizabeth, and Debby, who shared their tender charges with me and were patient with me when I asked for more time with them. Equal gratitude is due to all of the rest of the kitten caretakers who answered a stranger's call and coaxed, herded, and played so spontaneously. I cannot forget my debts to Lynne at the Milo Foundation for opening her gates to all of my projects, and to Barbara at the Mendocino County Humane Society for her support, as well. I also need to thank my friends, human and animal, for sustaining my body and brain with walks, dinners, generous opinions, and laughter during the last year while kittens and puppies consumed me. And lastly, I wish I could find a way to let all the kittens who overcame their fear of the strange, flashing human know how grateful I am for their cooperation, candor, and charm.*